MW00718092

YOU
are not
YOUR
OWN

BECOMING

GOD'S

STEWARD

Mike Armour

**COLLEGE PRESS
PUBLISHING COMPANY
Joplin, Missouri**

CONTENTS

STUDIES FOR SMALL GROUPS

Welcome to a new book series from College Press. The *Studies for Small Groups* series is designed for simplicity of use while giving insight into important issues of the Christian life. Some, like the present volume, will be topical studies. Others will examine a passage of Scripture for the day-to-day lessons we can learn from it.

A number of possible uses could be made of this study. Because there are a limited number of lessons, the format is ideal for new or potential Christians who can begin the study without feeling that they are tied into an overly long commitment. It could also be used for one or two months of weekly studies by a home Bible study group. The series is suitable for individual as well as group study.

Of course, any study is only as good as the effort you put into it. The group leader should study each lesson carefully before the group study session, and if possible, come up with additional Scriptures and other supporting material. Although study questions are provided for each lesson, it would also be helpful if the leader can add his or her own questions.

Neither is it necessary to complete a full lesson in one class period. If the discussion is going well, don't feel that you have to cut it off to fit time constraints, as long as the discussion is related to the topic and not off on side issues.

As the first volume in *Studies for Small Groups*, College Press is happy to present this four lesson study in Stewardship (which is much more than just finances), *You Are Not Your Own*.

YOU ARE NOT YOUR OWN

"Mine! Mine!" As toddlers, every one of us has voiced this declaration of ownership. You would expect Christians to outgrow such selfishness, wouldn't you? But, when churches across our affluent nation struggle to meet budgets, when ministries languish for lack of volunteers, there must be some vestige of childishness. *You Are Not Your Own* is a probing review of what the Owner's manual, the Bible, teaches about stewardship. A healthy understanding of biblical stewardship will remedy the problem of childish priorities.

What is a "steward?" A steward is simply a manager. Our English word translates the Greek word, *oikonomos*, probably a combination of *oikos* (house) and *nomos* (law or rule). The stewards who appear in New Testament stories are managers in a private position. It was a term used of a city treasurer or figuratively of administrators or ambassadors of "divine things." The concepts of planning, administrating, ordering, and regulating are key to understanding the meaning of stewardship. Often stewards in the Bible were slaves, but not all slaves were stewards. Stewards had the abilities and character to be assigned to positions of special trust.

Christian stewardship consists of conscientious living as well as unselfish giving. We need to assimilate the concept of being entrusted with the management of "the things of God." Stewardship is a matter of responsibility and accountability for our total conduct. God demonstrates his confidence in us by investing his inventory of tangible and intangible things with us. Stewardship is a matter of ownership — "I have been bought with a price and I own nothing." Therefore, only God has the right to set our daily priorities. Our goal is to discover a Christlike balance in our lives. To understand God's perspective on "success" is to have a proper understanding of what matters most to God. In these lessons we will rediscover two measures of true character. Our attitude toward money has always been an accurate standard by which we can measure. A second test is how we view unearned gifts from God.

Growing up in Christ (Col. 1:28) involves continually improving our stewardship. These four lessons will help us to grow by becoming more like Christ as trusted managers of his possessions. Few studies will be more rewarding than one which establishes God's ownership of our lives and our surrender to his Lordship. If you are ready to begin the adventure, commit yourself to learn *"You Are Not Your Own!"*

1
ONE

BOUGHT
WITH A PRICE

Every Christian is a steward. Peter urged that realization upon us when he wrote,

As each one has received a special gift, employ it in serving one another, as good stewards of the manifold grace of God (1 Peter 4:11).

From years spent with Jesus, Peter knew that themes of stewardship figured prominently in the Master's teaching.

- The parable of the talents recounts how three men were judged, based on the discharge of their stewardship (Matthew 25:14-30).

- The lesser-known parable of the minas (or pounds) relates a similar story about three stewards, two of them trustworthy, one of them not (Luke 19:11-27).

- Luke 16 tells of a shrewd, unprincipled steward who swindled his master for self-serving purposes.

- And Jesus compares vigilant disciples to stewards who remain attentive to their responsibilities, even when their master is away on an extended journey (Mark 13:34).

Gospel stories about stewards distinguish carefully between faithful and unfaithful service. Those lessons are vital for us. *The New Testament insists that as stewards, we must be trustworthy above all else* (1 Corinthians 4:2). What, then, does our stewardship entail? What does it mean to be a steward?

We cannot answer those questions by looking at people called "stewards" today. Labor unions have "shop stewards." Some race tracks refer to their governing council as "stewards." Aboard luxury liners stewards serve the passengers, while in the air, flight attendants (once known as stewardesses) perform a similar function. But those notions of stewardship are far removed from what Jesus had in mind when he used the term.

STEWARDS AS SLAVES

Stewards in biblical times were often slaves who, despite their bondage, possessed exceptional learning and ability. Many had once been people of rank and status. Perhaps bankruptcy had reduced them to slavery. Indebted families were commonly sold at auctions and the income used to satisfy creditors. Others were enslaved as a result of war. The Romans offset the cost of military campaigns by selling captives as slaves. These included men and women from all social strata.

People of wealth regularly procured such experienced, highly-trained slaves for positions of special trust. These "slave-stewards" might be placed in charge of the owner's children, his business, or portions of his estate. Their enslavement notwithstanding, these stewards had sweeping responsibilities.

The New Testament insists that as stewards, we must be trustworthy above all else.

To be sure, not all stewards were slaves. In the parables of Jesus we find both bond-servants and free

10

men serving as stewards. But the doctrine of Christian stewardship draws on the analogy of the steward enslaved to his master.

- "You are not your own," Paul reminded the Corinthians. "You have been bought with a price" (1 Corinthians 6:19-20).

- He referred to himself and his fellow-workers as *douloi* (bond-slaves) of Jesus (Philippians 1:1).

- He pressed the Romans to consider themselves "freed from sin" and "enslaved to God" (Romans 6:22).

It is hardly fashionable for Christians to think of themselves as slaves. We prefer the word "servant." It is softer in tone and far less demanding.

It is hardly fashionable for Christians to think of themselves as slaves. We prefer the word "servant." It is softer in tone and far less demanding. In our language servants are wage earners who negotiate their working conditions and are free to seek other employment. They yield some prerogatives to their employer, but otherwise retain basic control of their lives. Perhaps that explains our preference for the word "servant." We are not yet ready to relinquish total control to Christ.

To call ourselves "bond-slaves," however, confronts us with the probing question, "Who owns my life?" The first principle of Christian stewardship is to realize that "I am not my own; I have been bought with a price." But Jesus has not made me his bond-slave to demean me. He instead wants to entrust me with splendid responsibilities. That is why he emphasizes my stewardship.

THE QUALITIES OF A STEWARD

In the ancient world not every slave could be made a

steward. Many lacked the aptitudes and the strength of character which the function required. From the parables we learn that good stewards were:

- trustworthy
- self-starters
- always aware of their accountability
- diligent in carrying out their master's expectations
- ready to give a reckoning at any moment

These same qualities, of course, are hallmarks of Christian conduct. That is why Jesus borrowed so many stewardship analogies when he taught about discipleship. For him stewardship encompassed one's total existence and how it was managed.

Unfortunately we have not retained that emphasis. Christians today rarely hear of "stewardship" apart from financial contexts. More often than not, sermons on stewardship center on budgetary shortfalls and the need for greater contributions. We have reduced Christian stewardship to the issue of how we use our money.

Nor must we neglect the financial implications of stewardship. But it has implications which are equally urgent in other arenas of life. *Properly understood, stewardship is a matter of Christian living, not just Christian giving.*

STEWARDS AS MANAGERS

Properly understood, stewardship is a matter of Christian living, not just Christian giving.

The New Testament word for "steward" literally means "one who manages a household." Since Roman households tended to be quite large, including perhaps dozens of slaves in addition to an expansive family, household man-

12

agement was no small duty. Stewards were preeminently managers.

But we must be careful when we describe stewards this way. If we think of them as managers in the modern sense, we invite misunderstanding.

> The first principle of stewardship is acknowledgment that "I am not my own." The second principle is recognition that "nothing I have is my own."

- Stewards who were slaves had none of the prestige and social status we associate with executive positions.

- They were perceived primarily, not as "being in charge," but as "being charged with" particular duties.

- Unlike top management today, which often "owns the business," the steward owned nothing. What he managed belonged entirely to someone else.

Thus, if the first principle of stewardship is acknowledgment that "I am not my own," the second principle is recognition that "nothing I have is my own." In the words of the Psalmist:

The earth is the Lord's, and everything in it,

The world, and all who live in it (Psalm 24:1).

From that perspective, there is not one thing which truly "belongs" to me. I may speak of having possessions, abilities, or family and friends. But they are not ultimately "mine." God has simply entrusted them to my stewardship. Because they are so dear to him, he has placed them in my hands for nurture and safe-keeping.

THE STEWARD'S SELF-ESTEEM

The Old Testament figure Job respected this principle in his oft-quoted statement, "The Lord gives, and the Lord takes away" (Job 1:21). His recognition that he ultimately owned nothing permitted Job's steadfastness in the wake of lost fortune, family, and health. Here was a man who refused to build his self-identity around a resumé or a list of assets. He knew he had maintained a righteous stewardship over the things God had placed in his care. Now that they were removed, he remained unshaken in his righteousness, certain that he had discharged his stewardship faithfully.

We must learn from Job — not the world — how to form a proper sense of self-worth. When I yield to the world's counsel, I seek my self-identity in possessions and achievements, in physical prowess or attractiveness. Doing so, however, leaves me vulnerable to whatever tragedy or reversal may lie ahead. If possessions, achievements, and good looks constitute my self-worth, then I have no value once they are gone.

But as a steward, bought with a price, my value (and hence my self-esteem) is unassailable. So passionately did God want me as his steward that he did not hesitate to make the purchase, even at the cost of his own Son. No change or misfortune can obliterate that reality. *Slaves with stewardship skills sold at a premium in the marketplace. But none ever commanded the price God paid for me.*

Armed with that basis for my self-esteem, I am prepared like Job to weather all the turns of fortune. Or to say with the apostle Paul, "I have learned to be content in whatever circumstances I am" (Philippians 4:11). Possessions, success, and prominence are no longer measures of my value. They are merely the portfolio God has entrusted to my care at a given moment. If he chooses to remove that portfolio and give

Slaves with stewardship skills sold at a premium in the marketplace. But none ever commanded the price God paid for me.

14

me responsibility for another, my fundamental worth as a steward remains unaltered. After all, whatever stewardship he gives me must be important, for he paid such a dear price to have me as a steward to begin with.

REFLECTING ON LESSON ONE

1. How could we define a "steward" in biblical terms?

2. What are the implications of being "slaves" for Christ?

3. How does it change our outlook and bearing to view ourselves as managers of our lives, not the owners?

4. What common themes recur in the parables of Jesus about stewards?

5. What qualities are associated with trustworthiness (or faithfulness) in a steward?

6. Explain why biblical stewardship deals with more than money and finances.

7. What do you consider the most challenging areas of stewardship in your own life?

2
T W O

SEEKING THE MASTER'S PRIORITIES

Have you ever taken inventory of what God entrusts to us? Many items on the list come readily to mind: our homes, our income, our physical bodies. In addition, God has entrusted us with

- a spiritual essence
- emotions and attitudes
- the gospel
- an upcoming generation of children
- the church
- opportunities to serve
- time
- imagination and creativity
- nature and the environment.

We could extend the list indefinitely. Moreover, each item on the list represents a stewardship responsibility. Only when we grasp that reality do we begin to sense the vast confidence God expresses in us when he makes us his stewards.

At first glance such confidence is frightening. How can I ever measure up to the expectation it implies? With such an extensive array of stewardship duties, how can I possibly attend to all of them?

THE MOTIVE FOR SETTING PRIORITIES

The answer, of course, is that God does not expect me to seize every stewardship opportunity with equal diligence. Jesus himself could not take advantage of every occasion for good.

- He withdrew from Capernaum, even though throngs of people wanted more time with him (Mark 1:35-39).

- Another episode found him slipping away to train his disciples, despite the multitude gathered to hear him (Mark 6:30-32).

Jesus had to decide each day which duties were of first import, which ones of second. His ministry demonstrates that *stewardship is a continual exercise in setting priorities.* We must balance the long-range against the short-range; the spiritual against the material; time alone against time with others. These choices are inescapable. If we do not make them ourselves, circumstances will make them for us. *All of us lead prioritized lives. The only question is who will set the priorities.*

Paul urged Christians to "make the very best use of time, because the days are evil" (Ephesians 5:16). Early English translations captured the literal meaning of his words when they rendered this verse, "Redeem the time." Redemption was the process of buying back something that had been alienated from its original owner. In the case of people, redemption meant purchasing the freedom of someone kidnapped or

17

enslaved. Paul's imagery suggests a world in which time has been estranged from God's intent. Evil daily subverts the course of righteousness, and the job of Christians is to reinstate time to its rightful use.

How Christians use their time, then, is not merely a practical concern. It is a *spiritual* concern. Jesus warned that we are accountable for "every idle word" (Matthew 12:36). If we must choose every word wisely, how much more so our involvements.

Given that urgency, how should Christians go about setting their priorities? The beginning point is to remember that we are not our own. We have a Master. We are slave-stewards of a Lord who owns us, absolutely. That means our first obligations are to Him. As his stewards, we have unique responsibilities that would not be ours outside his service.

For instance, Christians have a clear interest in promoting good government, safe streets and healthy neighborhoods. But our responsibility to the community exists whether we are a Christian or not. The same may be said of humanitarianism. Our obligation to help others springs from being their neighbor, not merely from being a Christian.

On the other hand, some duties do not pertain to us unless we are in Christ. While non-Christians may spearhead humanitarian efforts (for they, too, sense the obligation of neighborliness), they have no preoccupation with the well-being of the church. Or to cite another example, people outside of Christ often work to promote vibrant communities, but they have no concern about souls eternally lost.

All of us lead prioritized lives. The only question is who will set the priorities.

By contrast, both the church and the lost were overarching priorities for Jesus. He died for them both. *As his stewards, we betray our trust if the*

18

Lord's priorities are not our own. We can easily become so enrapt in humanitarianism that we never make time to promote the gospel. We can become so engrossed in the commendable task of "making the world a better place" that we shirk commitments and duties to the church. While helping others and strengthening the community are good works, even Christian works, they are not the Christian's primary calling.

As his stewards, we betray our trust if the Lord's priorities are not our own.

Someone might object that we are only following Christ's example when we hold out a helping hand or work for mankind's betterment. Surely such efforts are his priority for us. But this objection takes too narrow a view of his ministry. Yes, he went about feeding hungry people and healing the sick. And those episodes are indeed models for our ministry. But when it came time to die, Jesus did not shed his blood to fill empty stomachs or mend broken bodies. He went to the cross to save men's souls and to redeem his church.

This should not be understood as meaning that Christians are to forego societal involvement. The key is maintaining balance. Jesus himself said that we are to let our good works be seen among men, so that they may glorify the Father (Matthew 5:16). *Good works are essential. But works without witness fall short of our duty as stewards.* In the same way, being a good citizen but neglecting the church misses the Lord's mark for our lives.

THE METHOD OF SETTING PRIORITIES

When I critique my stewardship priorities, I must begin by listing those duties which would not be mine had Jesus not made me his own.

- How well do I keep those responsibilities at the forefront of my day?

- Are my weekly concerns congruent with his sacrificial priorities?

- Do my commitments and priorities go beyond those of my highly moral, conscientious neighbor who does not even confess Christ? In other words, am I confusing "being good" with being a good steward?

Even many Christians in the apostle Paul's immediate circle proved careless about making the Lord's priorities their own. "They all seek after their own interests," Paul wrote, "not those of Jesus Christ" (Philippians 2:20).

A second step in my stewardship assessment is to evaluate the unique gifts the Lord has given me. How am I employing them in direct support of his priorities? Jesus compared his ascension to a master who, departing on a journey, assigned each slave in his household a specific duty (Mark 13:34). Both Peter and Paul remind us that every Christian has distinctive capabilities, individualized by God, which set one steward's service apart from another's. Peter worded it this way:

> As each one has received a special gift, employ it in serving one another as good stewards of the manifold grace of God. Whoever speaks, let him speak, as it were, the utterances of God; whoever serves, let him do so as by the strength which God supplies; so that in all things God may be glorified through Jesus Christ (1 Peter 4:10-11).

What are the things I do best? Do I employ them fruitfully in direct support of the Lord's work? Or do I reserve those abilities almost exclusively for vocational or avocational interests? Have I surveyed my talents and gifts with an eye to identifying specific ways I might use them with greatest impact in God's kingdom? *Peter describes our giftedness as a product of*

Good works are essential. But works without witness fall short of our duty as stewards.

20

divine grace. Dare I abuse his grace by withholding from his service the very potential for effectiveness which he imparted to me?

A third set of concerns when I evaluate my stewardship is whether an honest observer could tell that I put spiritual matters first in my life.

Peter describes our giftedness as a product of divine grace. Dare I abuse his grace by withholding from his service the very potential for effectiveness which he imparted to me?

- How does the time I spend in Bible study and prayer contrast to the time I spend watching TV?

- If I must choose today between reading the newspaper or reading God's Word, which will win out?

- When I look at the time and effort I give to the church, how does that compare with the energy I expend on hobbies?

- Am I as diligent and dependable in my church work as I am in other organizations I belong to?

- How does my financial contribution to the Lord's work compare to the amount I spend on vacations, weekend outings, and entertainment?

A simple test might be this: *if I were accused of being a Christian and the prosecution entered my Day-Timer and checkbook as evidence, would they contain enough proof to convict me?*

A fourth step in examining my stewardship is to ask whose benefit I primarily seek. Returning once more to Peter's words, we find him saying that we are to exercise our gifts "as good stewards . . . so that in all things God may be glorified through Jesus Christ." The steward's preoccupation is not himself, but his master. A steward who abused those things entrusted to him, or consumed them for his own pleasure, stood condemned for betraying his trust (Matthew 24:48-51). Jesus called such a person a "wicked servant."

In a consumer age, we readily fix on biblical stories of material blessings given to righteous people. Too easily we begin to think of prosperity or success as a reward for our devotion. God's perspective seems altogether different. He often operates on the principle that "he who has been faithful in a little will be faithful in much" (Matthew 25:21). Any master, needing to entrust something of value to a steward, would look first for a person who had already evidenced trustworthiness. When God blesses us, then, we should see it not so much as reward, but as an indicator that he believes us ready for broader stewardship. Having seen us discharge our duties faithfully as stewards over "a little," he now entrusts us with much more. But his objective for us remains the same — to be effective stewards.

If I were accused of being a Christian and the prosecution entered my Day-Timer and checkbook as evidence, would they contain enough proof to convict me?

REFLECTING ON LESSON TWO

1. The opening paragraph of this lesson lists several areas of stewardship responsibility. What others could we add to the list?

2. How did Jesus handle his priorities?

3. What are some similarities between the priorities of Christians and non-Christians relating to the community?

4. What guidelines would you offer a person in maintaining a balance between long-term endeavors and responding to short-term opportunities?

5. How do spiritual gifts relate to stewardship?

6. How does God's perspective on material blessings differ from the perspective of our consumer-oriented society?

7. What unique stewardship responsibilities do we have as Christians which would not be ours if we were unbelievers?

3
T H R E E

ONE KEY TEST
OF STEWARDSHIP

There were many types of stewards in the ancient
world. Some managed entire estates. Others were
entrusted with the rearing and training of the master's
children (Galatians 4:1-2). But the parables of Jesus
focus almost entirely on stewards responsible for
money and property.

Why did Jesus borrow his examples from such a narrow
range of stewardship duties? Perhaps it is because
themes of personal integrity figured so prominently in
his parables. In the first century nothing tested a person's integrity more deeply than financial stewardship.
It was a world which transacted business either through
barter or by direct payment in hard currency. Either
way, opportunities for pilferage presented themselves
daily. Accounting systems were rudimentary, at best,
with few checks and balances and limited "paper
trails." Thus, a dishonest steward, armed only with a
little daring and cunning, could line his pockets well.

Then, as now, money was one of the most corrupting
influences in society. Fortunes amassed by graft were
commonplace, especially among publicans (Roman tax-

collectors). Handling vast amounts of money seemed to go hand in hand with compromised integrity. Thus, trustworthiness as a financial steward was an excellent barometer of a man's true character. If he managed wealth without violating his trust, one could presume his faithfulness in other duties, too.

If he managed wealth without violating his trust, one could presume his faithfulness in other duties, too.

THE HEART OF MANAGING MONEY

The same is true today. What we do with our money is a good litmus test of our stewardship. Christians cannot buy their way to heaven, of course. But supporting the Lord's work consistently and generously is an excellent indicator of overall stewardship priorities. Jesus said "For where your treasure is, there your heart will be also" (Matthew 6:21). The opposite is also true. Most people invest their treasure where their heart is already anchored. When a person is reticent to contribute financially to help the cause of Christ, the problem may well be a heart not yet in that cause.

People often react as though it is somehow unspiritual for the church to talk about finances and giving. Nor is their reaction always unfounded. Churches, as surely as individuals, can be self-serving in the way they use money. Financial scams in the name of Christian ministry have been all too frequent in recent years. Even nonbelievers decry such carnality.

But excesses and wrongdoing do not invalidate the basic principle that supporting God's work financially is a distinctly spiritual duty. *The New Testament is replete with exhortations for Christians to practice liberality in giving.* Here is just a sampling of passages.

Do not neglect doing good and sharing; for with such sacrifices God is pleased (Hebrews 13:16).

Instruct those who are rich in this world not to be conceited or to fix their hope on the uncertainty of riches, but on God, who richly supplies us with all things to enjoy. Instruct them to do good, to be rich in good works, to be generous and ready to share . . . (1 Timothy 6:7-18).

Let our people also learn to engage in good deeds to meet pressing needs, that they may not be unfruitful (Titus 3:14).

Let him who steals steal no longer; but rather let him labor, performing with his own hands what is good, in order that he may have something to share with him who has need (Ephesians 4:28).

I testify that according to their ability, and beyond their ability, [the Macedonians] gave of their own accord, begging us with much entreaty for the favor of participation in support of the saints, and this, not as we had expected, but they first gave themselves to the Lord and to us by the will of God. . . . Just as you abound in everything, in faith, utterance, and knowledge and in all earnestness and in the love we inspired in you, see that you abound in this grace also. . . . For you know the grace of our Lord Jesus Christ, that though he was rich, yet for your sake he became poor, that you through his poverty might become rich (2 Corinthians 8:3-5, 7, 9).

Now this I say, he who sows sparingly shall also reap sparingly; and he who sows bountifully shall also reap bountifully. Let each one do just as he has purposed in his heart; not grudgingly or under compulsion; for God loves a cheerful giver. . . . Now he who supplies seed to the sower and bread for food will supply and multiply your seed for sowing and increase the harvest of your righteousness; you will be enriched in everything for all liberality, which through us is producing thanksgiving to God. For the ministry of this service is not only fully supplying the needs of the saints,

The New Testament is replete with exhortations for Christians to practice liberality in giving.

26

but is also overflowing through many thanksgivings to God. Because of the proof given by this ministry they will glorify God for your obedience to your confession of the gospel of Christ, and for the liberality of your contribution to them and to all (2 Corinthians 9:6-7, 10-13).

The ability to give generously is reassurance that we are not fixing our security and trust on "the uncertainty of riches," but on the certainty of God's supply.

PRINCIPLES FOR CHRISTIAN GIVING

In this series of admonitions, scattered throughout the New Testament, the Holy Spirit points to numerous principles which underlie Christian giving.

- Giving is directly equivalent to the sacrifices Jews brought to the tabernacle and temple.

- Sacrificial giving pleases God.

- The ability to give generously is reassurance that we are not fixing our security and trust on "the uncertainty of riches," but on the certainty of God's supply.

- Meeting pressing needs (financially, as in other ways) is a major aspect of being fruitful in God's service.

- One of the motivations for earning more is to be in a position to aid those who are without means.

- When we are willing to be deprived in order to aid good works financially, we imitate the example of Christ who gave up his splendor and became poor for our sake.

- Giving, done cheerfully and bountifully, can be undertaken with assurance that God, seeing such liberality, will generously supply what the giver needs for his or her own sustenance.

- Exceptional giving results in an outpouring of thanksgiving to God on the part of those whose needs are met, along with expanded glory being given his name.

THE SACRIFICE IN GIVING SELF

Most of these passages are exhortations to give, not examples of individuals who practiced this grace. But in one case, the generosity of certain early Christians was so striking that it lives on in Scripture. Paul says of the believers in Macedonia that they begged fervently to have a part in the collection he was gathering for famine-starved saints in Jerusalem. He uses a variety of phrases in 2 Corinthians 8:1-5 to describe their giving:

- They gave in a time of great affliction in their own walk with the Lord.
- Not only did they give, they did so with an abundance of joy, despite the fact that these Greek Christians were themselves impoverished.
- Their giving was not merely according to their ability, but beyond their ability.
- There was no compulsion placed upon them, but rather they gave of their own accord.
- They pleaded "with much entreaty" to participate in this special collection.

Such determined generosity is striking. Paul even acknowledged that it amazed him that Christians who had been in the faith only a few months could show such mature commitment. How had it happened? The apostle explains it with these words: *"they gave themselves first to the Lord."*

They gave themselves first to the Lord.

This brings us once more to the theme of our first lesson. We are not

28

our own. We belong to a master who possesses our very being and all that we have. These Macedonians, having grasped what that concept implied, viewed nothing they had as their own. Although impoverished themselves, and persecuted at the same time, they did not cling to the limited financial resources at their disposal. Instead, they looked upon whatever they had as something entrusted to their care by God. If he now needed to use some of these resources to relieve suffering Christians elsewhere, they were ready to redirect his resources accordingly.

Interestingly, Paul never speaks of the size of their contribution. He does mention the overflowing "wealth of their liberality." Given their poverty, they may not have matched what prosperous Corinth was able to do. *But the size of the gift was not the issue. The heart behind their giving is the matter of note.* Jesus laid this principle firmly in place as he watched people of substance make sizable offerings at the temple in Jerusalem. When a poor widow, possessing only two mites (less than a day's wage), contributed what she had, Jesus said hers was the greatest gift of the day (Mark 12:41-44). Proportionately she had given far more than all the rest. In fact, she gave all that she had.

This woman's example notwithstanding, Scripture nowhere demands that we give everything we have to support the work of God's kingdom. Paul did not require wealthy Christians to give away everything, but merely to be generous (1 Timothy 6:17-18). The issue is a matter of balance. We are to be prudent in the way that we use our money, neither wasting it nor hoarding it. We properly use what God supplies when we meet the necessities of life; but we must guard against letting mere "wants and wishes" becoming redefined as necessities. Masters fully understood that their stewards had to eat and clothe themselves, and that such provision would come from the master's supply. It was only when stewards went beyond that point and began to use the master's goods selfishly that they fell under condemnation.

REFLECTING ON LESSON THREE

1. Why did Jesus use examples from finances so often in his teachings about stewardship?

2. In what ways is our financial stewardship a helpful indicator of how well we are exercising our overall stewardship duties?

3. How important was giving to meet the needs of others according to the writers of the New Testament? Cite some examples.

4. What guidelines can we use to determine whether our savings accounts are indeed prudent provision for the future as opposed to evidence that we have placed our sense of security in "the uncertainty of riches"?

5. The Old Testament required Jews to tithe. Christians, by contrast, are told simply to set aside a sum of money in keeping with their income (1 Corinthians 16:2). Without the tithing standard, how does a Christian set an appropriate level of giving?

6. What are some biblical examples which would support the idea that the size of the gift is not the main issue in giving?

7. How does a Christian determine how much of his or her giving will go to the church as opposed to other charitable and appropriate works in the community?

4
F O U R

GIFTS OF GRACE

Jesus told several parables about a master, leaving on a lengthy journey, who entrusted items of great worth to his stewards. In his absence the stewards were to use that bounty to promote their master's interests.

Those stories should be considered the backdrop for the New Testament doctrine of spiritual gifts. Both Peter and Paul describe the diversity of gifts which God imparts to believers. *But these gifts are never for personal aggrandizement or glory. Instead, we have a stewardship duty to employ them on behalf of the Lord's commitments.* In a passage we have noted in earlier lessons, Peter writes:

> As each one of you has received a special gift, employ it in serving one another, as good stewards of the manifold grace of God (1 Peter 4:10).

THE MEANING OF GIFTS

At first it seems a bit strange that Peter does not urge us to be good stewards of the gift, but to act as stewards of God's grace. His phrasing makes more sense, however, when we realize that this verse masks a clever word

32

play which English cannot replicate. Peter's term "gift" (*charisma*) is a derivative of the Greek word for "grace" (*charis*). What the apostle says is that we are all stewards of *charis*, because each of us has received a *charisma*.

The *charis* Peter has in mind here is not so much saving grace as it is God's kindness in giving spiritual gifts to believers. Because we receive differing patterns of spiritual gifts, Peter describes this grace as "manifold." It takes a variety of forms. Whatever the form, however, Christians must invest it diligently, as dutiful stewards.

As if to underscore the unique nature of these gifts, the New Testament uses *charismata* (the plural of *charisma*) to distinguish them from other gifts. In Matthew 2:11, where the wise men bring gifts to Jesus, the word is *doron*. The saving gift of grace is also denoted by *doron* (Ephesians 2:8), as are the gifts men make to God in sacrifice (Hebrews 5:1).

But when biblical writers speak of a spiritual gift, they consistently choose *charisma*. In Scripture this unique word for "gift" always appears in a context of how God's grace has worked to empower the believer. *Charisma* is literally "a grace thing."

When we come to a passage about spiritual gifts, we need to keep this connection with grace in mind. Only once does the Greek New Testament append the word "spiritual" to *charismata* (Romans 1:12). In most cases *charisma* (or *charismata*) is unmodified. When first century readers saw it standing alone that way, their mind went first and foremost to grace (*charis*), not the Spirit (*pneuma*).

This is not to diminish the Spirit's work through the

gifts. Paul clearly teaches that the Spirit is their author (1 Corinthians 12:8-9). And occasionally the New Testament uses *pneumatikos* (literally, "a thing of the Spirit") as a synonym for *charisma* (1 Corinthians 12:1; 14:1). *But from the vantage of stewards, we need to perceive spiritual gifts as an act of grace. They are neither a reward nor an entitlement.* They are a result of God's kindness, an expression of his eagerness to see his stewards succeed.

THE PURPOSE OF GIFTS

Since we have received them in a stewardship capacity, our duty is to use them for the Master, not ourselves. Paul reminded the Corinthians that each Christian "is given the manifestation of the Spirit for the common good" (1 Corinthians 12:7). He thus echoes Peter's admonition to employ spiritual gifts "in serving one another."

Throughout the New Testament, indeed, there is a consistent insistence on taking the focus off of self in the exercise of spiritual giftedness. Our longest biblical discourse on the gifts is a result of Paul's disappointment that the Corinthians were misusing their gifts to call attention to themselves. "When you assemble," he told them, "each one has a psalm, has a teaching, has a revelation, has a tongue, has an interpretation. Let all things be done for edification" (1 Corinthians 14:26).

From the vantage point of stewards, we need to perceive spiritual gifts as an act of grace. They are neither a reward nor an entitlement.

The word "edification" means "to build up." It highlights our individual responsibility to strengthen one another (Romans 15:2). In fact, the only time the New Testament speaks of using a gift for self-edification, it does so only to discourage the practice (1 Corinthians 14:1-4).

Thus, to paraphrase Paul's counsel to Christians in Corinth, we have been given spiritual gifts to serve others, never ourselves. Many so-called "charismatic" circles today overlook this principle when they urge Christians to seek "the gift of tongues" as a sign of the Holy Spirit's work in their lives. Paul, by contrast, told the Corinthians that "tongues are for a sign, not to those who believe, but to unbelievers" (1 Corinthians 14:22).

Throughout the New Testament there is a consistent insistence on taking the focus off of self in the exercise of spiritual giftedness.

On the other hand, the same verse describes prophecy as a "sign for believers." Paul amplifies that thought later when he writes, "One who prophesies speaks to men for edification and exhortation and consolation (1 Corinthians 14:3). Or as he adds in the next verse, "One who prophesies edifies the church."

Every spiritual gift mentioned in Scripture has one of two designs: it is either like prophecy, for use in edifying the church; or like tongues, for evangelizing the lost. Many were useful in both. Some gifts were apparently temporary (1 Corinthians 13:8). Others, we presume, were permanent endowments to the church, since Scripture says only that certain ones were temporary, not all of them.

Not only does the distribution of gifts vary within the church from age to age, the patterns of gifts may change over time in the life of an individual. Paul encouraged Corinthians to seek gifts beyond those they already had (1 Corinthians 12:31). Gifts, once received, might not be retained. Paul himself, once blessed with extraordinary healing powers (Acts 19:11-12), was compelled at a later date to leave a co-worker behind because of ill health (2 Timothy 4:20).

Beneath this variable dissemination of gifts lies the operative power of the Holy Spirit. "The same Spirit works all these things, distributing to each one individually just as he wills" (1 Corinthians 12:11). As the apostles went about their work, God confirmed their credentials "both by signs and wonders and by various miracles and by gifts of the Holy Spirit according to his will" (Hebrews 2:4). In this verse the word "gifts" is not *charismata*. It is instead a term for "distribution" or "measure." Spiritual gifts are what the Holy Spirit measures out to each worker. This reminds us of the parable of the talents, where the master distributed different amounts of money to each individual. Not everyone receives the same measure when it comes to spiritual giftedness; but like those stewards, we are to use whatever we receive for the same purpose — the master's business.

THE DISCOVERY OF GIFTS

This then raises the obvious question of how one determines his or her pattern of gifts. There are two models of spiritual gifting in Scripture. The more familiar one is found in Romans and 1 Corinthians. Spiritual gifts, as described there, are exceptional powers which grant the believer absolutely new capabilities. The less familiar model is found in Exodus, as Moses prepared to build the tabernacle. God instructed him to bring together the skilled artisans and craftsmen who would undertake the work. God then filled them "with the Spirit of God, in wisdom, in understanding and in knowledge and in all craftsmanship" (Exodus 35:30-35).

A spiritual gift may not always be

> Every spiritual gift mentioned in Scripture has one of two designs: it is either for use in edifying the church or for evangelizing the lost.

36

something new, therefore. It may some-
times be a divine empowerment that
permits far greater effectiveness with
the talents we already possess. Thus,
even if I have no evidence that I
have one of the gifts mentioned by
Paul, that does not mean that I have
nothing to offer the causes of edification and evangelism. God may be
waiting for me to invest those abilities which are already mine. What
he has in mind may be special
enhancement of my native talents
so they can be particularly fruitful in his service.

A spiritual gift may not always be something new. It may sometimes be a divine empowerment that permits far greater effectiveness with the talents we already possess.

*Thus, the starting point in discerning one's spiritual
giftedness* is a self-inventory of skills and abilities. Do I
already have a desire to employ those in ways that have
a direct bearing on the work of the church? If not, the
first issue I must deal with is not the matter of spiritual
gifts, but motivation. If I am not eager to use present
capabilities in the work of the kingdom, what purpose
do I have in seeking others? When our motives are
right, it is appropriate to seek greater giftedness. Paul
clearly makes that point. But we should not pursue
added gifts unless we yearn to use them for non-self-
serving purposes.

*Once my self-inventory is complete, I need to begin
using those capabilities* in direct support of the church's
mission. I should experiment, trying different avenues
of service until I discover where I seem to be the most
fruitful. Sometimes I will discover that I am not particularly effective at something, even though I long to excel
at it. When that happens, I must remember that non-
giftedness in a given area is no reflection on my spiritu-
ality. The Holy Spirit does not distribute gifts as
rewards or as tokens of recognition, but according to his

perception of overall needs at a moment.

Of course, if I am not gifted in an arena of service which appeals to me, it would be appropriate to pray for gifts I lack. Christians frequently develop unprecedented fruitfulness through the avenue of prayer. But if the Spirit chooses to withhold the gifts I seek, I must remain ready to serve elsewhere, using what he has already imparted to me. Again, stewards do not set their own life agenda. They take what the master places in their hands and do the work he commissions them to perform.

And finally, I must also recognize that my pattern of gifts may change over the years. Just because someone is a fruitful teacher at one time does not mean he or she will be effective forever. The Spirit may choose to take what a person has learned through years of teaching and utilize it in some fresh new ministry elsewhere. If we make the mistake of building our self-identity around our effectiveness with a particular gift, it may prove difficult to relinquish that service graciously when the time comes to do so.

When fruitfulness seems to fade in an area where we have previously enjoyed fulfillment and success, we need to open our eyes to other opportunities which the Spirit may be placing before us. Who knows? A complete new pattern of gifts may be making its way into our life. Whole new vistas of service may be unfolding before us. As good stewards we are always at the Master's call, eager to perform accountably wherever he asks us to work.

> When fruitfulness seems to fade in an area where we have previously enjoyed fulfillment and success, we need to open our eyes to other opportunities which the Spirit may be placing before us.

38

REFLECTING ON LESSON FOUR

1. Discuss the meaning of the New Testament word *charisma*.

2. What constitutes effectiveness in the exercise of a spiritual gift?

3. What are the two broad categories of spiritual gifts discussed in the New Testament?

4. What are some ways that the distribution of spiritual gifts has changed throughout church history?

5. What should we do if we do not believe we have one of the spiritual gifts mentioned by Paul?

6. In his parables, Jesus repeatedly chastises "fearful stewards." In the exercise of spiritual gifts, what are some fears we may have to contend with?

7. In what practical ways can we help one another identify our individual spiritual gifts?